SHORT · SCENIC

# HARROGA

**&**

## KNARESBOROUGH

**PAUL HANNON**

## HILLSIDE PUBLICATIONS
20 Wheathead Crescent
Keighley
West Yorkshire
BD22 6LX

First Published 2009

© Paul Hannon 2009

ISBN  978 1 870141 92 5

*The sketch maps are based on 1947 OS one-inch maps and earlier OS six-inch maps*

Cover illustration: Ripley
Back cover: Markenfield Hall
Page 1: Almscliff Crag
(Paul Hannon/Hillslides Picture Library)

Printed by Steffprint
Unit 5, Keighley Industrial Park
Royd Ings Avenue
Keighley
West Yorkshire
BD21 4DZ

# CONTENTS

# INTRODUCTION

The rolling countryside surrounding Harrogate is a delightful, easily accessible area to enjoy gentle country walking. Based in or close to the lower Nidd Valley this rich tapestry of patchwork fields, cosy stone villages and stately old houses holds a wealth of interest, from landmark rock outcrops to colourful woodland and elegant parkland. Norman castles at Knaresborough and Spofforth contrast with the splendour of Markenfield Hall, Rudding Park and Newby Hall. Idyllic villages like Kirkby Overblow, Ripley and Follifoot are found in amongst natural wonders such as Almscliff Crag and Spofforth Pinnacles.

The Nidd and, fleetingly, Ure flow wide and calm in these tranquil lower reaches, each offering charming riverbank paths: the Nidd Gorge proves a livelier exception. The celebrated floral spa town of Harrogate and its extraordinarily colourful partner Knaresborough are major tourist attractions in their own right, and make excellent bases for discovering ancient green lanes, old railway lines, inspiring churches and welcoming village pubs.

Whilst the route description should be sufficient to guide you around each walk, a map is recommended for greater information: Ordnance Survey 1:25,000 scale maps give the finest detail, and Explorers 289, 297, 298 and 299 cover the walks. Many of the walks are accessible by use of public transport, with buses radiating to numerous villages.

*Left: Newby Hall*                    *Knaresborough Castle*

## USEFUL INFORMATION

·Harrogate Tourist Information (01423-537300)
·Knaresborough Tourist Information (0845-3890 177)
·Ripon Tourist Information (0845-3890 178)
·The Ramblers
2nd Floor, Camelford House, 87-89 Albert Embankment, London SE1 7BR (020-7339 8500)
·Traveline - public transport information (0870-608 2608)

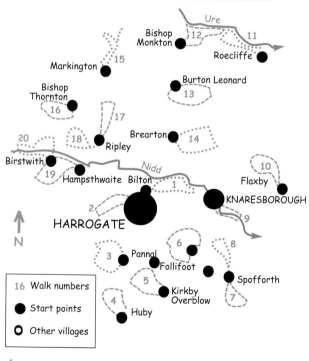

# HARROGATE &
## KNARESBOROUGH

## 20 Short Scenic Walks

*Ure*

Bishop
Monkton

12

11

Roecliffe

Markington

15

Burton Leonard

Bishop
Thornton

16

13

17

Brearton

14

20

18

Ripley

Birstwith

19

Hampsthwaite   Bilton

*Nidd*

1

Flaxby

KNARESBOROUGH

9

HARROGATE

2

↑
N

Pannal

6

8

3

Follifoot

5

Spofforth

Kirkby
Overblow

7

4

Huby

| 16 | Walk numbers |
| ● | Start points |
| O | Other villages |

# A RECORD OF YOUR WALKS

| WALK | DATE | NOTES |
|------|------|-------|
| 1 | | |
| 2 | | |
| 3 | | |
| 4 | | |
| 5 | | |
| 6 | | |
| 7 | | |
| 8 | | |
| 9 | | |
| 10 | | |
| 11 | | |
| 12 | | |
| 13 | | |
| 14 | | |
| 15 | | |
| 16 | | |
| 17 | | |
| 18 | | |
| 19 | | |
| 20 | | |

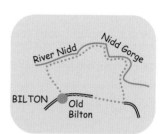

**4¹₂ miles
from Bilton**

**First-rate wooded
river scenery
between Harrogate
and Knaresborough**

*Start Old Bilton (GR: 314575), car park on old railway line
on Bilton Lane, reached from A59 Skipton Road, Harrogate
Map OS Explorer 297, Lower Wharfedale/Washburn Valley
or Explorer 289, Leeds/Harrogate/Wetherby/Pontefract*

Modern housing at Bilton on the edge of Harrogate ends
abruptly at the former railway that served Pateley Bridge, Ripon and
points further north. A plaque also marks the course of a narrow-
gauge mineral line that branched westwards from here between
1907 and 1956 to carry coal to Harrogate Gasworks. Leave suburbia
behind by heading away on the contrastingly quiet continuation of
Bilton Lane. Almost at once on your left is the Gardeners Arms at
Old Bilton. This is what a real pub looks like, with an array of cosy
rooms supplied from a simple serving hatch. Behind the pub in 1980,
Franklins Brewery started producing locally crafted ales, one of
the pioneers of the small brewery revolution.

Continue along the road, which swings up and around past
a caravan site to enter more open surroundings. Eventually losing
its surface at a padlocked gate, pass through and remain on the
rougher continuation, soon reaching a footpath signed through a
gate on the left. Turn along this to a stile into the Woodland
Trust's Nidd Gorge Woods. The main path heads away left with the
springtime scent of wild garlic, running for some time along the top
of the wood. Ultimately, at a waymarked fork, take the right
branch slanting grandly down the partly open bank to the foot of
the wood, with the Nidd waiting below.

At the very bottom turn upstream past immediately splendid surrounds with craggy walls opposite. This riverside path remains underfoot for some considerable time, during which you pass a long, tall footbridge over the river, then a spell well above its winding bank before dropping back down. Various sections of the path have been reinforced by boards, and there is even a little spell by sandy beaches as you leave and then re-enter Woodland Trust land. Just before reaching a weir that served the smart old mill opposite, an old way (the second of two) drops to the river-bank, serving an old ford. The path turns up this hollowed way, now with wooden steps, to a path junction: bear right to a signed junction just around the corner, and take the right branch slanting steadily back to the river, emerging by the weir. The house on the opposite bank is the former Scotton flax mill, dating from 1798.

Resume upstream just as far as a footbridge on a side-stream. Across, take the left fork ascending the steep bank away from the river, emerging into a big field corner. Take the path bearing right, following the wood edge to meet the old railway line, greeted just before it by the sight of the 100-foot tall arches of the Nidd Viaduct. Completed in 1848, this carried the old line over the Nidd Gorge: though closed in 1967, some freight traffic continued for a further two years. Turn left on the old line, on which a popular path runs on a minor cutting. This leads you back to the start.

*Pub sign at the Gardeners Arms, Bilton*

*4 miles
from Harrogate*

**Delightful gardens
and woodland crags
on the very edge
of Harrogate**

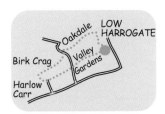

*Start* Pump Room, Low Harrogate (GR: 298553), car parks
*Map* OS Explorer 297, Lower Wharfedale/Washburn Valley

From the Pump Room cross the road into Valley Gardens
and follow the left-hand path to a cafe. Almost half of Harrogate's
88 mineral wells are found hereabouts. Beyond the cafe take the
main path up the centre of the gardens. Rising by a wall, it continues
to a junction at a war memorial. Bear right on the woodland path
left of the cross, entering the Pinewoods. This runs pleasantly on
to meet Harlow Moor Road. Directly opposite, a broad path heads
back into trees, soon reaching a large grassy clearing. Passing along
its right side the firm path heads back into trees, soon emerging
to run along the edge of the woodland, with open views to the right.
Passing Pinewood Farm the path drops onto Crag Lane facing Harlow
Carr Gardens. The premier botanic gardens in the North of England
are open to the public on a site developed as a spa in the 1840s.

Go right 100 yards and turn left to the Harrogate Arms,
the 19th century hotel for the adjacent spa. In the corner below,
in front of the gates of a study centre, turn right through a small
gate and a path sets off into trees. This runs a good course above
the little ravine of a stream. Further, a guidepost marks a junction
with the Harrogate Ringway walk, now followed for some time. Turn
right on the Ringway, winding steeply down to a footbridge. Going
briefly downstream, the path quickly slants up the bank to more
open woodland of birch, bracken and shrubs to a fence corner. As
the way splits, remain with the right-hand path ascending with the
fence: on levelling out a wall takes over. The path runs grandly on
to quickly reach the edge of the gritstone buttresses of Birk Crag.

The path rises above the near side of the rocks to a junction. Turn left to remain above the outcrops on an initially enclosed way. After Birk Crag House things open out, with opportunities to stand on the crags for views over wooded Oakdale to rolling fields. The path continues, and after the last outcrops drops to a junction. Remain on the upper path which stays near the wood top above further crags. Gentler surrounds take over as the path drops to a broader, level path. Continue on this to reach Harlow Moor Road. Cross and descend the pathway left, past the first side road to one part way down, after the last house. This broad access road doubles back right above woods, becoming broader then surfaced. Marching on through well-heeled suburbia, stay alert for a snicket on the left. This drops between fences to re-enter woodland. Turning right, it soon zigzags down to the bottom to resume downstream with Oak Beck.

Further along, the other side opens out to reveal a golf course. As the bank narrows the path ascends steps, then along the wood top outside gardens before being deflected from the valley by a fence. The path forges on through tapering trees to emerge onto suburban Oakdale Glen by the golf club. Abandon the Ringway, turn up onto Oakdale and cross to an enclosed path up steps through trees onto suburban Kent Road. Turn briefly right then left on Kent Avenue. St Wilfred's imposing church stands at the end, where turn left on Duchy Road. Take the next right, Clarence Drive, and remain on this as it curves down to re-enter Low Harrogate at the edge of Valley Gardens, with the start just down to the left.

Pump Room, Harrogate

*4¹2 miles*
*from Pannal*

**A genteel ramble round
the fields and streams
of Pannal utilising the
Harrogate Ringway walk**

*Start Village centre (GR: 305516), roadside parking*
*Map OS Explorer 297, Lower Wharfedale/Washburn Valley
or Explorer 289, Leeds/Harrogate/Wetherby/Pontefract*

From St Robert's church with its 15th century tower, follow
the road to the bridge after which go right on Mill Lane. At the end
a path runs on by a millpond, then into woodland with Crimple Beck.
This runs through trees to dwellings at the yard of an old cornmill.
Go ahead to a gate and along a broad path, still in greenery. This
emerges onto a road at the edge of Burn Bridge, with the Black
Swan pub just to the right. From a stile opposite, an enclosed path
heads away onto another road. Cross to another enclosed path, and
a stile at the end puts you into a field. Advance on the hedgeside
to a corner gate/stile, and a path rises to the edge of The Warren,
a wooded knoll. Through a gate turn right up to the brow, still outside the wood. Drop to a gate into the wood, and a path drops
steeply to leave by a bridge. An enclosed way rises onto a road.

Go briefly right to a bridle-gate and along the fieldside.
A gap at the end sees a path cross a footbridge on Crimple Beck
and into a field. A path ascends a slim enclosure, through a kissing-
gate and up onto a road. Go briefly right and up an enclosed path
to emerge into a large field. Rise up the centre to a stile, and along
a short fieldside to another. Continue to a corner stile and over
again to one in a kinked corner. Bear right to a corner one, and down
the hedgeside to a path junction at the bottom in front of a beck.
Turn sharp left here, slanting back on a grassy way up the bank to

the previous hedge. Continue on the fading track's obvious course, rising very gently in tandem with the beck over to the right. From a hedge corner ahead advance through a stile and on a fieldside to another, then along to a stile in the fence ahead. Turn sharp left to a little gate onto a road and go right to a junction. Leaving the Ringway, turn right on Whinney Lane past the Squinting Cat pub. Just after the dip and at the bend take an enclosed path outside a garden. A bridle-gate at the end puts you into a field, where a path rises to one opposite. Cross sports fields to a rough access road at the end, leading out to a suburban road. Cross and go right for a couple of minutes, then take an enclosed path on the left. This remains enclosed throughout its winding course to another street. Turn right to a junction, then left through more leafy suburbia.

Across a bridge in a dip take a path right, on an enclosed course between gardens and wooded stream, emerging into a field. Bear right as it tapers to merge into an enclosed path, and along to a stile onto a road end. Back on the Ringway turn right down the rough continuation to a bridge. Climbing the steep wooded bank, fork left through a gateway and a good enclosed path runs outside the tree-lined beck, ultimately down to a path crossroads beneath Almsford Bridge. Noting a more direct, parallel fieldpath from the kissing-gate, take a stile in front and accompany Crimple Beck towards Pannal. When the beck turns left the path goes right with a tiny stream to join the direct path. From the bridle-gate this crosses a field centre, and from the next stile the field tapers to a stile into the churchyard, emerging at the other side onto the road.

*Landscape at Beckwith*

*3½ miles
from Huby*

**Easy walking
to a celebrated
Wharfe Valley
landmark and viewpoint**

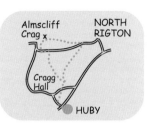

*Start* Huby (GR: 275474), roadside parking, Weeton Lane
*Map* OS Explorer 297, Lower Wharfedale/Washburn Valley

Huby is a scattered village with some nice corners. From the rail station cross the main road to Strait Lane. Follow this up to the village edge, and look for a cross-path. Go right on a narrow snicket between houses to fork in front of a field. The left branch remains enclosed behind gardens to reach a house: follow its drive out onto Crag Lane. Cross to an enclosed green way rising away, quickly swinging right into a field with an impressive prospect of Almscliff Crag. Bear right along the bottom, through a kissing-gate and on to the far end. From a kissing-gate drop through the wood corner to a stone slab on a tiny stream and another gate. Ascend outside the wood to another stile. A 'preferred permissive route' takes a more circuitous course right with the fence, avoiding the house. The public path runs on the hedgeside and along to the drive at the front of imposing Cragg Hall (Holly Hill on map), and over a stile to pass another house with a gate onto another drive. Cross to a gate into a farmyard, and on to emerge into the field beyond.

Cross the field to a stile in the hedge opposite, and on through a small scrubby field to a stile and tiny stream. Slant left to a stile in a rising hedge and maintain this line, aided by marker posts to slant across a number of fields to a wall-stile onto North Rigton's Crag Lane. Pause for a fine Wharfe Valley panorama then turn right to a stile by a seat. Minutes further is North Rigton, featuring the Square & Compass pub and village stocks on a little green. From the stile, meanwhile, double back left up to a stile in the facing hedge.

Cross a drive and head away with a wall on your right, drawn by close-at-hand Almscliff Crag. After two triple squeezer-stiles rejoin a right-hand wall running to a stile into the crag's environs. A path forms to rise to the rocks, ascended easily from this side to the crest of the major outcrop, High Man. Stop when you get here!

This major Wharfe Valley landmark is prominent in views from all around the district. Sat among neatly packaged fields, it is a popular venue for climbers: the rough gritstone offers scores of named routes. The extensive panorama embraces the full girth of Rombalds Moor, along with lesser neighbour Otley Chevin. A section of wall between the two main bluffs of High Man has a stile in it to descend to the base of these main crags. Immediately below are further outcrops known as Low Man, with a path along the base. Go left here, above or below the crags, round to a corner where an enclosed footway descends to Cragg Farm. A wall-stile leads onto the road, where turn left down to a small group of houses. After the last take a gate on the right, dropping to one just below. Slant to a stile opposite then turn down the hedgeside. From a stile in the bottom corner descend a field centre to a gate in the hedge below, and down another hedgeside to a gate where a firm track forms. This drops down outside a plantation to rejoin the outward route at Cragg Hall, from where retrace opening steps.

*At Almscliff Crag*

*3³⁄4 miles
from Kirkby Overblow*

**Steady rambling giving
fine open views from the
surrounds of an attractive
hilltop village**

Start *Village centre (GR: 325491), roadside parking*
Map *OS Explorer 297, Lower Wharfedale/Washburn Valley
or Explorer 289, Leeds/Harrogate/Wetherby/Pontefract*

Kirkby Overblow is a pleasant village on an exposed ridge
between the Wharfe and the Nidd. From the Shoulder of Mutton
cross to a lane on the top side of the Star & Garter. Keep on into
the churchyard, passing All Saints church with its 15th century
tower to a stile at the far end. Entering a garden, cross to a stile
onto a drive, then bear right to a wall-stile into a field corner. Take
the inviting enclosed pathway right, running over a brow and down
to emerge onto narrow Walton Head Lane. Go briefly right then
take an enclosed path on the left. This descends a delightful
course, passing a pond to emerge onto a road opposite Brig Hall,
former almshouses. Turn left up the road's broad verge, and along
the gentle brow. Big views look north-east to the Hambleton Hills
skyline. Starting a gentle decline, leave by a stile on the left. Cross
the pasture to a gateway in the wall near the far corner, then on
again to a gate in a fence. Just behind is a stile onto the A658.

Cross with care to a like stile in the hedge opposite, and
cross the field to a gap in the hedge corner ahead. New views look
over the Crimple Valley. Head away with the hedge on your right
just as far as a gateway (not used), then turn sharp left and cross
the field down to a stile in the fence opposite, below a wood. Head
away again, joining the right-hand hedge to approach a housing
development at Walton Head Farm. Over a stile advance on the slim

field outside the houses to a gate ahead, then bear left down the field to a stile and a footbridge in the fence. Head away with the hedge on your left: over to the right rises the great boss of Almscliff Crag. From successive stiles at the end bear right to a facing stile to gain access to the verge of the A658. With a wary eye on descending traffic, cross to a stile opposite and escape along the field. This same course is maintained to approach a house, but with the hedgeside to your right. The path bears left round the garden wall to a stile further on, crossing the front garden to join the drive out onto Walton Head Lane.

Cross to a stile and bear left over this small enclosure to another, then ascend the long fieldside rising away. By the time the brow is reached you have big views south over the Wharfe Valley to Danefield and Otley Chevin: Almscliff Crag rises impressively above Huby. Pass through a stile on the brow and descend the other side to a corner stile. Cross to another just to the left, then cross a couple of field tops followed by an open field plagued by seepage beneath Wareholes Well, a centuries-old holy well. From a bridle-gate at the end a nice climb by a hedge leads to a kissing-gate atop the brow. Resume above the hedge on your right, on a long fieldside above a wooded bank followed by a longer one. With the church tower getting closer, further stiles lead to a small corner gate at the walk's early path junction. Pass through the stile on the right into the garden to finish as you started through the churchyard.

*Kirkby Overblow*

*3¹2 miles
from Follifoot*

**Rambling by old railway,
country lane and spacious
parkland on the edge of
a charming estate village**

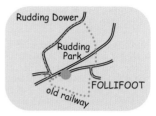

*Start* Truncated section of Pannal Road alongside A658
junction west of village (GR: 333523), roadside parking
*Map* OS Explorer 297, Lower Wharfedale/Washburn Valley
or Explorer 289, Leeds/Harrogate/Wetherby/Pontefract

Advance to the road's abrupt end at the last house,
where an enclosed bridleway continues parallel with the main road.
This drops to an underpass by which you shall return. For now
advance straight on, rising slightly then swinging sharp left to run
to a junction at a hairpin bend. Here leave the bridleway and go
straight ahead through a kissing-gate. A firm track remains underfoot as you head along the deep trench of a railway cutting, with
wooded banks to either side and new tree-planting. This was the
LNER's Church Fenton & Harrogate branch which ran through
Wetherby: it closed in 1964, courtesy of the infamous Dr Beeching.
Further on, leave by a broad path that slants left up to
a kissing-gate. An inviting green track doubles back left along the
fieldside. Just ahead part of Follifoot becomes visible, with the
considerably more distant Hambleton Hills on the edge of the
North York Moors beyond. Bear right at the end, just as far as a
broad gap on the left giving a clearer picture of Follifoot below.
The track descends the fieldside, swinging right at the bottom and
becoming enclosed as it crosses Horse Pond Beck. Remain on this
splendid hedgerowed way as it zigzags into the village. When it
becomes a firm access lane at some houses, use a low stile on the
left to resume as a tightly-enclosed footway between gardens,
turning right at a junction to emerge onto the main street.

18

Follifoot is a little village of great character, with a Post office/shop and two pubs, the Radcliffe Arms and Harewood Arms. Stocks survive on the side of the green, which bears an old cross. The imposing Rudding Arch fronts an old driveway to Rudding Park. Turn left to the T-junction and right on Plompton Road to the 19th century church of St Joseph & St James. Your path takes the stile into the end of the churchyard, though first go a few steps further to see the restored, circular pound that housed stray livestock. A stile at the bottom of the churchyard sends you down a hedgeside to a stile onto the A658. Cross to another and a short path drops down onto a firm track.

You are now in part of the large estate of Rudding Park. Currently a conference centre and hotel, the present house dates from the 1820s. Go right then quickly left on the track as it runs alongside a sturdy wall, immediately entering a golf course. Remain with this wall all the way to the very end, much of the way on a track apart from the corner where you will find a fence-stile. Bear right with a short drive at Rudding Dower out onto Rudding Lane. Turn left for a long, steady rise on broad verges outside Rudding Park. At the top it bends left to run to a junction just short of the A658. Turn right on Pannal Road, leaving at the first chance by an enclosed track on the left before the first house. This drops to the underpass: to the left is Prospect rail tunnel entrance. Emerging to join the outward route, turn left to finish as you began.

*Rudding Arch, Follifoot*

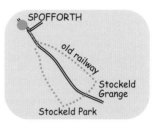

*3¹2 miles
from Spofforth*

**A former railway leads to stately parkland on the edge of an historic village**

*Start* Village centre (GR: 363510), roadside lay-bys
*Map* OS Explorer 289, Leeds/Harrogate/Wetherby/Pontefract

Spofforth is an attractive, historic village dominated by its castle ruins dating from the 13th century: home of the Percys since Norman times, their departure to build the mighty Alnwick Castle in Northumberland in the early 14th century left Spofforth to decay. Spofforth has pubs, a Post office and shop, while All Saints church has a solid 15th century tower and a 14th century monument to Sir Robert de Plompton. Leave the road through the village by its junction with the main road at the Castle pub, noting an old milestone outside. Head south on the A661 Wetherby road. Reaching suburban East Park Road bear left along it, continuing to the end where a path forms to run to the start of the railway path.

With the aid of cycling charity Sustrans, this old line has been transformed into a footpath and cycle route known as the Harland Way. Its delightful course traces the trackbed of the former Harrogate-Wetherby railway. Originally the York and North Midland Railway's Harrogate branch, it later became the LNER's Harrogate & Church Fenton branch, before its closure in 1964 courtesy of Dr Beeching. Advance along here on a charming stroll through sylvan surrounds. After rather less than a mile you encounter a cross-path at a set of wooden seats on the left. Here leave by turning right, where an inviting, hedgerowed green way rises to a stile, then slant left up the field to reach Stockeld Grange. A stile admits to the farmyard, then rise up to the right of the buildings on the short drive onto the A661.

Cross with care to the lodge opposite and set off on the verge of the main drive into Stockeld Park. When it swings left to the house, advance straight on through archetypal parkland, noting a folly hidden in trees on the right. A little further you pass a tree-shrouded pond in a hollow on your right. Stockeld Park is a splendid house completed in 1763 for William Middleton. In the 1890s it was acquired by the Foster family of Black Dyke Mills in Bradford, and though still occupied it also opens for various functions.

Joining a rougher driveway coming in from the house, you attain the best glimpse of it. Advance to a gate into trees. After a couple of minutes the trees on the right end: turn through a gate and head away on a fieldside track outside a wood. Views expand as the wood ends, and a very gradual decline makes for a grand stride until the track ultimately curves around to the right. This could be followed but would leave a longer road walk back into the village. Instead, take a stile on the left part way around, and with the church tower ahead cross an enclosure of Christmas trees to a stile opposite. Slant down across the field to a gate in the far corner, then cross to a stile ahead. Cross straight over a narrow field to a gate, then bear right up to a corner stile outside modern housing. Just yards round the corner to the right is a hidden stile, from where follow a short rough way out onto an access road. Go briefly right, then left on Park Mount back out to the main road opposite the Railway Inn. Go left to finish as you began.

Spofforth Castle

21

*4¼ miles
from Spofforth*

**A super beckside ramble
leads to some
unexpectedly outstanding
rock formations**

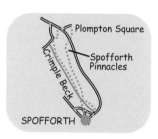

*Start* Village centre (GR: 363510), roadside lay-bys
*Map* OS Explorer 289, Leeds/Harrogate/Wetherby/Pontefract

For a note on Spofforth see page 20. Leave the road through the village by one opposite the shop, running past a green to swing right past the church onto the A661. Go left on a footway as far as the bridge on Crimple Beck. Across, turn upstream on a path largely adhering to the flood embankment. Stay close to the beck to pass a footbridge after the last building (the old mill), which you will cross to finish the walk. Resume along the bank and maintain this course all the way. Over to the right several massive gritstone sentinels stand island-like in the fields, outliers of Spofforth Pinnacles. Better examples are seen further on, and all these will become better known on the return.

The path faithfully traces the beck upstream to reach a stile onto a road alongside a bridge. Don't use the stile but turn right on a thin path parallel with the road, and as the road swings away maintain this line alongside Brown Hill Wood to a stile onto the A661. Cross and follow the verge briefly right to turn left up an access road to reach a pair of lodges at Plompton. Not on route, but just after the lodges, a gate points the way to Plumpton Rocks. Situated on private land for which an entry fee is payable, the grounds are normally open weekends and Bank Holidays, March to October. Laid out long ago as pleasure grounds by Daniel Lascelles, this 30-acre park boasts a fine collection of gritstone outcrops all interwoven with shrubs, woodland walks and an attractive lake.

At the lodges turn right up the road to the houses at Plompton Square. Turn sharp right along the first row, continuing at the end on a short enclosed path to a stile into a field. Bear right to drop to a gate in the far corner. Re-cross the A661 to a stile, and a nice path heads away with the wall outside the wood to a stile on the gentle brow. This overlooks the Crimple Valley as you emerge into the splendid surroundings of Spofforth Pinnacles, a modest version of Brimham Rocks. Of two paths heading away, the public path bears left along the edge of the area. A more inviting path drops left through the heart of this scene, savouring more fully this fascinating collection of gritstone monoliths amid bracken. At the far end, outside the farm at Braham Hall, the slim main path passes through an old fence-line into a more standard enclosure.

Keep on to a minor knoll, then drop left of a small marsh, passing another isolated outcrop. From a small gate at the end bear right to follow the hedge on the bottom of the enclosure, passing a pond not seen until the last moment. Keep on through a gateway and beneath further rocks to a stile at the end. Part way along the next field take a gap in the hedge, over a stone slab bridge. Cross the tapering field to regain the embankment of the outward route. Turn left the short way back to the footbridge, and this time cross it to follow an enclosed path past the old mill. You also cross the deep, dry channel of a former cut on a stone-arched bridge and out onto Mill Lane. Look back to appraise the substantial three-storeyed former Spofforth Cornmill. Turn right and follow up into the village, going either right for the castle, or left for the start.

*At Spofforth Pinnacles*

*4 miles
from Knaresborough*

**Knaresborough's fascinating
riverside features fill
this easy stroll through
a craggy wooded gorge**

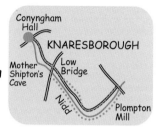

*Start High Bridge (GR: 345571), Conyngham Hall car park
Map OS Explorer 289, Leeds/Harrogate/Wetherby/Pontefract*

At High Bridge is the entrance to Mother Shipton's Cave.
Your route takes the town side of the bridge, on the narrow road of
Waterside past the Worlds End pub. Its colourful course passes
under the rail viaduct and past boat landings to reach Low Bridge.
Cross the road and resume on Abbey Road. Tall cliffs to your left
feature the House in the Rocks: completed in 1791 it comprises
four vertical rooms. Just past it is the Chapel in the Crag, a way-
side shrine of 1408, its entrance guarded by a carved knight.

Resume on the road, soon between tall cliffs and the Nidd.
As the cliffs end take a steep path up the wooded bank. Climbing
to a junction, double back left beneath a higher cliff to climb steps
to a broad, level path. Turn right and remain on it for some time on
Crag Top, squeezed between housing and the steep wooded bank.
Ignore a path dropping away and remain on this leafier path. Reaching
more open surrounds with new housing set further back, ignore the
broad, firm path and remain on the old one by the fence above the
bank. Further along, alongside scrub, this descends the bank, passing beneath further cliffs to slant back down to the road. Resume
on here past gnarled golden cliffs to reach a traffic impasse at
some red sandstone houses on the site of a 13th century priory.

As the road enters more modern housing a gate on the
right marks the entrance to St Robert's Cave, just a few steps
down into trees overlooking the river. A hermit for almost forty

years until his death in 1218, his pilgrims included King John: the cave hewn from the cliff was his original chapel, the base of its successor evident outside. The road joins Wetherby Road on the edge of town. Turn right over Grimbald Bridge and immediately upstream on the other bank. An old drive runs to an open area between Plompton Mill Farm and an old cornmill. Past the last of the caravans a path squeezes up the wooded bank onto a splendid knoll beneath a sandstone crag. From here you look down on another weir supplying a mill with a waterwheel on the opposite bank. The path drops to the edge of the same caravan site, but within a few steps it keeps right to run outside the site above the steep wooded bank.

Dropping back to the river this fine path traces the Nidd through splendid woodland. After passing a massive house opposite, you emerge into a sloping field. The fenced path crosses it well above the river to a driveway. Ignore its climb left, and go straight on past a couple of houses, as a path squeezes beneath a massive limekiln at the base of low crags. Back onto the riverbank the path resumes beneath steep woodland with enviably sited houses across the water. A short pull towards the bank top precedes a drop back down to a garden wall, and on to emerge by an interesting house. Follow the lane, Spitalcroft, past other houses and out onto the road on Bland's Hill. Turn down the footway past the Mother Shipton Inn back to Low Bridge and retrace steps to the start.

*Knaresborough*

*4 miles
from Flaxby*

**Very simple rambling
through the fields
to visit an
attractive village**

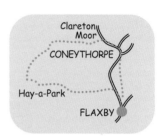

*Start* Village centre (GR: 395579), roadside parking
*Map* OS Explorer 289, Leeds/Harrogate/Wetherby/Pontefract

Tiny Flaxby boasts a number of attractive cottages. The side road leaving the small, triangular green was originally the A59, no less, heading for York (via the A1, whose muffled noise might be a constant backdrop to the walk). Head north on the through road (Shortsill Lane), leaving the village. Passing the old school room on a bend, a straight section offers a wide verge as you stride out. Just after Spring Bank farm drive on the right, go left on Castle Farm drive. This runs through the fields to its objective, where a tall, red-brick house stands beyond the barns. Go right between barns into the yard, then left. With more traditional barns on the left, the drive turns sharp right towards a house: ignore this and take a gate straight in front. An inviting, embanked old way heads off along the fieldside, through a gate at the end and between fields to transform into a cart track running to Mill Farm.

Pass between the buildings and out along the surfaced drive to reach a junction. Turn right the short way to Hopewell House Farm, keeping right of all buildings to the end. Bear right on a rising track to a field corner and keep right on the main track as it forks: this runs to another fork in front of a forlorn stone gatepost. Keep left, still on the main way which surmounts a gentle ridge and continues, part enclosed, then on a fieldside towards a red-brick barn. Just past this it swings left to reveal the sprawling farm of The Hollies just ahead. Halfway along the last fieldside before it, a clear, signposted path doubles back right, across the field centre to a corner. From a hedge gap on the right maintain this cross-field course to another gap, and on again across a larger field. Towards the end it turns left to accompany a hedge, now as a superb green track heading for Clareton Moor Farm. Passing through a gate keep on the track which swings left of all of the buildings and out via a gate onto a road.

Turn right and follow this road for a few minutes to enter Coneythorpe, soon reaching the centre of this tiny village based around an open green. On it stands the village pump, while facing it is the Tiger Inn. Green Lane heads away from the pump, but you take the one to its right, a short-lived drive. Waymarks indicate the start of a small snicket to the right, running between gardens to a stile and on again to emerge via a tiny footbridge on an even tinier stream into the corner of a field. Turn right along the hedgeside to a corner stile between useful boardwalks, then cross a rising field, crossing the Spring Bank drive and on above a modest bank to a stile at the end. Extensive views look right over the Knaresborough and Harrogate area. With Flaxby on the brow just ahead, a super fieldside way heads off to join the road at the village entrance. Advance on to finish as you began.

*Village pump, Coneythorpe*

*4 miles*
*from Roecliffe*

**Relaxed walking**
**on the lush bank of**
**the wide-flowing**
**lower Ure**

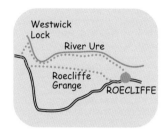

*Start* **Village centre (GR: 376659), roadside parking**
*Map* **OS Explorer 299, Ripon & Boroughbridge**

Close to the historic town of Boroughbridge, Roecliffe is a very attractive village with houses set back from spacious greens. The red-brick school sits in the middle, sporting a clock tower with a canopied spire and weathervane. There is also a popular pub, the Crown Inn, while St Mary's modest church of 1843 has a small bell turret and a Jacobean pulpit. An enclosed path leaves the village alongside the church, then along a brief track into a farmyard. Turn sharp right to a gate into a welcoming open pasture. Head away left, soon reaching a vantage point revealing the River Ure flowing wide and calm at your feet.

Drop to the Ure's bank and turn upstream. That is really the last instruction until leaving the river, for the route is never in doubt. A number of stiles, gates and some small footbridges are encountered, in a variety of fields and scattered trees, all pretty good stuff. The river undertakes a steep curve as you pass through Cherry Island Wood, and soon after re-emerging you arrive at Westwick Lock. Here the short-lived, canalized Westwick Cut helps craft avoid an unnavigable weir just upstream. This is a splendid spot for a break, with the red-brick Lock House alongside. At one time a ferry used to ply the river here, while the Island between the two watercourses is popular with anglers. A short stroll along the modest length of the dead-straight cut is firmly recommended. as far as the other end where it joins the Ure.

The River Ure (anciently the Yore) is the principal river of the Yorkshire Dales. It rises on the bleakest of moorland 2000ft up above Mallerstang and Garsdale Head, and flows through such favourite haunts as Hawes, Bainbridge and Aysgarth before leaving the National Park near Middleham and taking in the market town of Masham and the historic city of Ripon. After absorbing the rivers Cover, Burn, Skell and Swale it meets its end a few miles short of York where it transforms into the Ouse.

Leave the river here for the anglers' car park which is sited up to the left, from where a short access road runs out through the fields onto Boroughbridge Road. Turn left for just a few minutes, and just beyond Westwick Hall Farm, a footpath is signed through a gate on the left. Bear right across the field to look down on the river. The path runs to enter the bridleway of Sheaflands Lane, which is enshrouded in greenery. Turn left on this for a super walk, initially along the top of Cherry Island Wood, with the river just below, then more openly to the farm at Roecliffe Grange. Keep straight on the verges of its access road to emerge onto a road by a nursery. Roecliffe is just a couple of minutes to the left.

*Barge on the River Ure at Roecliffe*

*4¾ miles
from Bishop Monkton*

**Delightful riverside
walking close by the
Newby Hall estate**

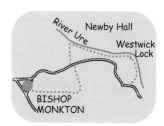

*Start* Village centre (GR: 329662), roadside parking
*Map* OS Explorer 299, Ripon & Boroughbridge

Bishop Monkton is a lovely village enhanced by a stream
running through the centre. The church of St John the Baptist
boasts a tall spire, and there are two pubs and a shop. Leave by
heading south from the Lamb & Flag along the main street in the
company of the stream. At the end turn left opposite the Masons
Arms, along an enclosed rough lane, Ings Lane. A modest brow soon
affords a glimpse of the White Horse of Kilburn on the Hambleton
Hills beyond the Vale of York. Remain on its dead straight course
all the way past a house and on to a fork: as the main way turns
sharp right, keep straight on down a softer track to the bottom
just below, where it fades. A leafy enclosed footway takes over,
swinging left and running a fine course before emerging into a field.
Keep straight on over a stile ahead and along the hedgeside, which
terminates just short of a gate onto Boroughbridge Road.

Turn right, the road's early stages subject to occasional
flooding. At the second sharp bend turn left on the access road to
Westwick Lock. This runs through fields to an anglers' car park
overlooking the lock where the canalized Westwick Cut helps craft
avoid an unnavigable weir upstream. Alongside is the red-brick Lock
House. Resume in the brief company of the cut to rejoin the Ure.
Grand rambling ensues through sheep pastures, while Newby Park,
the spacious grounds of Newby Hall, occupies the opposite bank. A
miniature railway is seen before the house itself appears, straight
across the water and neatly framed by its gardens.

Newby Hall is one of Yorkshire's great stately homes, open to visitors though not from this bank of the river! The elegant red-brick house dates from 1705, built for Sir Edward Blackett from the profits of his Tyneside collieries. The spacious grounds are an attraction in their own right, comprising some 25 acres and featuring a sculpture park. One or two moist moments may be encountered before entering Holbeck Wood. The path crosses a footbridge on the dead-straight cut of Holbeck, then emerges at a kissing-gate to briefly leave the river. Bear left to a surfaced road alongside a couple of nissen huts and concrete bases, the remains of a Second World War military training area that also featured a narrow gauge railway. Alongside is a section of widened river where engineers erected pontoon bridges to be tested by tanks.

Advance briefly along the road to its demise where it bends back left, and keep straight on the rougher road to end in trees at a gate ahead. This next field is your last: look back for a glimpse of the front of Newby Hall. At the end is a bridge on a sidestream: don't cross, but from a kissing-gate on the left a field-side path heads away from the river. At the end it becomes a firm, embanked way to emerge back into a field. Again it runs along the side to a gate, then to a small gate onto Boroughbridge Road half a mile east of the village edge. Turn right to return, passing the Mechanics Institution of 1859 and possibly bearing left to conclude alongside the duck-dabbling stream by the old Main Street.

*Bishop Monkton*

*4¹4 miles
from Burton Leonard*

**Charming rural ways
linking two
unassuming villages**

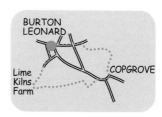

*Start* Village centre (GR: 327638), roadside parking
*Map* OS Explorer 299, Ripon & Boroughbridge

Burton Leonard is a colourful village grouped around an arrangement of greens, with a red-brick Methodist church, school, Royal Oak pub, Post office/shop and village pump in a shelter on the lower green. Head east from the centre, past St Leonard's church and the Hare & Hounds pub, leaving the village on Mill Lane. From the brow are views east to the Hambleton Hills: visible is the White Horse of Kilburn, along with a much closer, equally celebrated Yorkshire landmark, Ripon Cathedral. Go straight over a crossroads and down with a verge, until a turning branches right. Take this, and remain on this access lane to a cattle-grid at the end of a wood. At this path crossroads the access road bears right towards Crow House: your route is a lesser track straight ahead. Beyond a gate/stile in a fence the track improves, running on past another wood edge to approach a big modern barnyard. While the track swings right to ford Holbeck, you have the option of a footbridge.

Now turn right to a gate/stile onto the access road, and go right on it, briefly, passing a pond. Level with Well House, ignore its drive rising away and instead take a gate on the right. Head away outside the wood, holding to the fence on your left to rise pleasantly to a cluster of houses at Copgrove. Advance through a stile and on to a snicket behind, between hidden gardens to emerge onto an access road, St Mongah's Lane. Go straight ahead on this suburban drive to emerge at a road junction alongside a church. The little church of St Michael & All Angels has a bell-cote and Norman origins. Turn right on the verge, leaving the village and ignoring a branch left at a lodge. The verge leads all the way to your turning, where a surfaced way slants left after a directly ascending drive. This comes just before the road drops to bridge a lake. It is worth continuing to this point to appraise the splendid large lake, which with its swans makes a fine foreground to Copgrove Hall.

Your side branch, meanwhile, rises outside Dark Walk Wood, improves into a cart track and runs on to a bridle-gate onto a surfaced access road, Green Lane. Turn right on this, soon reverting to a cart track. The way drops to Robert Beck in trees. Don't cross, but take the branch left, which rises away slightly then runs a super course along fieldsides on the southern flank of the beck. A section midway is enclosed by hedgerows to eventually meet an access road. Turn right on this down the fieldside: towards the bottom take a track bearing right off the drive to a ford and footbridge on the beck by the house at Lime Kilns Farm.

Head away on the access road up and along to a junction with a through road at a triangular green: however, after the last house on the right you might detour via the Burton Leonard Lime Quarries nature reserve of the Yorkshire Wildlife Trust. A path ascends outside the garden then swings left to run a grand woodland course to where a branch right reveals the substantial walls of the old quarry. The continuing path runs on and gently up to rejoin the access road. At the junction go left on the road to emerge onto the top of the sloping High Green, descending back into the centre.

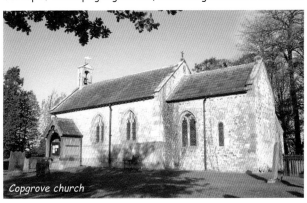

Copgrove church

*4 miles
from Brearton*

**Rural rambling linking
two lovely villages
on very good lanes
and tracks**

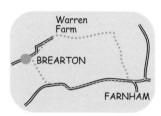

*Start* Village centre (GR: 322609), roadside parking
*Map* OS Explorer 299, Ripon & Boroughbridge

Brearton is a leafy, sleepy village retaining its pub, the popular Malt Shovel. Its modest little church of St John the Baptist dates from 1836 and looks down on the village green. Head east along the cul-de-sac village street's footway to the sloping green at the far end, which features stately beeches and a reed-

filled pond. Keep left at the green, and at a bend on the village edge take a gate on the right. Bear left on an invisible path which short-cuts a bend of the lane to a stile back onto it. Turn to the right along this traffic-free, hedgerowed way which terminates at an isolated house, with Warren Farm to the left. Advance on the continuing cart track, which ends at a gate ahead. Now cross the field on a faint green way, with Walkingham Wood to your left. Keep on to the narrower end to a gate onto a crossroads of bridle-ways in a few trees.

*The bridleway to Farnham*

Turn right on the enclosed green path, which runs a delightful course between hedgerows to reach stone-arched Shaw Bridge. Up the other side this quickly becomes Shaw Lane, leading along to shortly enter the centre of Farnham. Another laid-back village, Farnham is entered alongside a triangular, sloping green. Turn right to reach the church, which after a visit can be left by steps back down to the road. St Oswald's church is a fine building dating largely from the 12th century to the 15th century, when the tower was added.

Remain on the road, Stang Lane out of the village for a considerable stride of virtually a mile, partly with a good verge and then with woodland to the left as it runs a dead-straight course. Beyond a bend remain on the road until curving round to reach a junction alongside Lingerfield school. Here escape by a bridleway heading off to the right and running a tightly enclosed course between hedgerows. Emerging into a field at the end, advance along the hedgeside until it turns away: now advance straight on, curving gently left past some bushes to pass a fence corner and along a faintly embanked course to a bridle-gate ahead. This admits to a cart track which runs on between hedgerows to join Low Moor Lane. Go left on this as it improves its surface to emerge back into Brearton alongside the church and green.

*Farnham church*

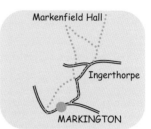

*3³⁄₄ miles
from Markington*

**A modest country ramble
with a classic green lane
and the major highlight of
a magnificent old building**

*Start* **Village centre (GR: 287650), roadside parking**
*Map* **OS Explorer 298, Nidderdale
or Explorer 299, Ripon & Boroughbridge**

Markington is an attractive village with two pubs, a shop and the church of St Michael the Archangel. From the village hall go west on the street past the Yorkshire Hussar pub and turn right on the Fountains Abbey road. After crossing Markington Beck bear right on a drive to a house, past which a kissing-gate admits to sports fields. Bear left past the pavilion, past the cricket pitch and keep left to find a path up a low bank behind goalposts. A thin path heads diagonally away along the right side of a hedge. From a gate at the end head away in nicer surrounds, picking up a faint green track running pleasantly on the fieldside to houses at Waterloo.

Pass along the front of the buildings, but without setting foot on the road turn left up a snicket to a stile into undergrowth. The path rises as a superb, hollowed way through woodland, and along to emerge onto a narrow road. Go right a few steps to take an old stile in the wall, crossing a field to approach Yarrows Hill farm. The Hambleton Hills form a distant skyline over to the right. On the edge of the yard, keep left of all buildings and rise left to a gate into a field. Bear right on the hedgeside to a corner stile onto a track. With Christmas trees all around advance to a stile just in front and resume on a grassy track to reach a stile into more plantings. A few yards left a poor track crosses to a wooded bank, bearing right beneath it to a corner stile onto Strait Lane.

Double back right on this slender bridleway, a lengthy route deep in greenery, slowly dropping down until it swings sharp right and broadens. This is the point to which you will return after a look at Markenfield Hall, visible across the fields. From a stile on the left a path crosses to a short enclosed section. Beyond a gate/stile it continues as a green track bound for the hall. At the end pass through a gate and turn right onto the drive, swinging left between outbuildings to the 16th century gatehouse guarding a bridge over a moat fronting the hall. Here you can gaze with awe at a magnificent scene, still a working farm and home. The hall is open to view on a limited basis, currently afternoons in early May and late June, though much can be seen externally. A stile to the right at the end gives an opportunity to appraise the great east window of the chapel from across the moat. This fortified manor house dates from 1310: long the home of the Markenfields, Sir Thomas saw an end to that when he played a major role in the Rising of the North in 1569: when this floundered the estate was forfeited.

Returning to Strait Lane go left, absorbing a broader track to emerge onto a road. Turn right and remain on this past Ingerthorpe Moor Farm and Waterloo to return to the village. Markington Beck is re-crossed in a lovely woodland setting. The road climbs into the village past the grounds of Markington Hall, a 17th century manor house featuring two great wings and numerous mullioned windows. Turn right along the road from which the hall can be appraised, passing the Cross Keys pub to conclude.

*Markenfield Hall*

*3½ miles
from Bishop Thornton*

**Two peaceful villages
are linked by the
flanks of the valley
of Thornton Beck**

*Start* Village centre (GR: 262633), roadside parking
*Map* OS Explorer 298, Nidderdale

Bishop Thornton is a peaceful village with two churches
and two schools: the church of St John the Evangelist is eclipsed
by the tiny Roman Catholic church of St Joseph: dating from 1809
it features Stations of the Cross that transform the plain interior
into an art gallery. From the junction head west through the village
and at a bend after the RC church gate, take a gate on the left and
pass right of farm buildings down to a stile. Head away, bearing
right to merge with a hedge along the fieldside. Towards the end
take a stile at a kink and resume on the other side. When the hedge
turns off, advance straight on to a kissing-gate onto a road.

Just a few yards left take a gate on the right and an old
green way descends the fieldside: ahead is the valley of Thornton
Beck. Through a gate at the bottom continue down a field centre:
at the bottom ignore a stile and turn right on the wallside. Part way
through the second field bear right, slanting gently up towards
houses ahead. A wall-stile admits to a short snicket, and onto a
road on the edge of Shaw Mills. Turn left past an old Wesleyan
Methodist Church to the village centre. The village grew as housing for workers at nearby High Mill, and takes its name from early
mill-owner Robert Shaw. The Nelson Arms closed in the 1990s, a
little short of two centuries of serving ale. The environs of the
bridge make a delightful floral display with old steps down to
Thornton Beck, so you'll just have to drink that in.

Across the bridge turn sharp right on the drive rising to Cow Gate Farm. Over to the right is the sizeable High Mill. After the drive swings left up to the house, advance straight on a short green way to its right. At the end turn right through a gate and on a fieldside track. Improving views look over this rolling valley to a Brimham Moor skyline. Adhere to this faint old way, ignoring a branch left as the way runs outside a wood. Through a gate at the wood end a thin path slants down across a large, sloping pasture. From a bridle-gate at the far corner head away with the wall, past a double spring just after which is a small gate in the wall. Through it a footbridge crosses Thornton Beck and a little path rises into a field. Rise past Beck House (Black House on map) to a bridle-gate onto the drive. This rises away to a T-junction, where turn right.

Passing a farm to a junction at the end, take the access road right to Hatton House Farm. Swing left between the buildings and at the end a cart track continues into a field. After a tiny enclosed section it continues as a gentler grassy way on a fieldtop. At the end it becomes enclosed to drop down to a junction at farm buildings. Ignore both options and take a gate on the left, to ascend a field to a stile hidden in the top corner. A thin path crosses a small, scrubby enclosure to a stile in the fence ahead. Cross the field diagonally to a corner stile, then head away to cross a bridge on a stream before continuing to a gate onto the bend of a road. Bishop Thornton is just two minutes along to the right.

*Shaw Mills*

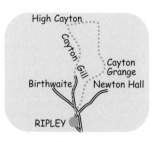

*4¹⁄2 miles
from Ripley*

**Easy walking from a
classic village through
an unfrequented and
richly wooded valley**

*Start* Village centre (GR: 284605), car park
*Map* OS Explorer 298, Nidderdale

Ripley was a market town in 1357, and seat of the Ingilby family since before that. Nothing here is without interest, though the castle is the major attraction. First sight is the imposing early 15th century gatehouse. Through its great arch are spacious lawns and a courtyard. The castle was largely rebuilt in 1555 and was much enlarged in 1780, though the old tower dates from less than a century after the gatehouse. After the battle of Marston Moor this Royalist castle supposedly received a visit from Oliver Cromwell, while his troops shot prisoners they had brought to the village. The lakes and deer park were laid out by Capability Brown and are open throughout the year. The castle is open at various times, daily in summer. For more on the village see page 42.

Head north on the main street past the Boars Head, and towards the end bear left on the sidelined main road: note the old milestone. At the end cross the B6165 and head off on steadily rising Birthwaite Lane. When it becomes unsurfaced keep on to a fork at a triangle. Bear right on a cart track, and over the cattle-grid just beyond, fork left on an inviting green fieldside track. This runs along the field top and past a wood. At the end ignore the track into woodland ahead, as the bridleway curves right to a brow with views eastwards across the Vale of York to the North York Moors.

The track slants down the wooded bank to a gate at the bottom onto the floor of Cayton Gill. Just a little further, it turns to cross this shallow valley on a modest, low-arched grass bridge over the stream trickling out of the marsh. All around are new plantings. Rising to a gate up the other side, a path bears left along the top of a planted bank before dropping briefly through trees at the end. The path then advances very pleasantly along the edge of this valley floor. Up to the right are the grassy remains of a barely discernible medieval village. Reaching a path junction in front of a wood at the end, turn right through the gateway and a little path rises into a field. This crosses to enter the farm at High Cayton.

Pass through and out along the access road to a major fork, where bear right. Ignore a right branch to Cayton Gill Farm and remain on the track which rises to a brow: its view features the Hambleton Hills, the ubiquitous Nabs Ridge wind turbines and of course Cayton Gill. The track then drops down to the houses at Cayton Grange. Pass straight through and along the access road heading away. This runs on beneath a wood, climbing to approach Newton Hall. At a cattle-grid beneath the house take a pair of stiles on the right, then slant very gently down across the field to the fence enclosing the wooded beck. Just beyond its corner use a footbridge to cross it. A thin path heads directly across the field centre to a corner stile, and on again to a bridle-gate in the hedge ahead, just right of the busy roundabout. Re-cross the B6165 to the footway and your exit point from the village is just to the right.

*The Gatehouse, Ripley Castle*

*3³⁴ miles
from Ripley*

**Easy rambling amid
some historic features
on the edge of
a classic village**

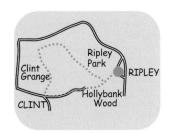

Ripley
Park

Clint
Grange

RIPLEY

Hollybank
Wood

CLINT

Start *Village centre (GR: 284605), car park*
Map *OS Explorer 298, Nidderdale*

Aside from its castle (see page 40), Ripley's village is an
attraction in its own right, with the Boars Head pub, shops, farm
museum and tearoom. This classic estate village was rebuilt by Sir
William Amcotts Ingilby in 1827, based on a French village of
Alsace Lorraine - note the town hall named the Hotel de Ville. The
medieval market cross has stocks alongside. The church was built
in 1400 but restored in 1862, and the Ingilby chapel has life-size
effigies of Sir Thomas and Lady Ingilby dating from around 1370.
In the churchyard is a pre-Reformation weeping cross: the far
from comfortably positioned sockets at the bottom cater for the
knees of penitent souls.

From the square follow the side road between church
and castle, losing its surface to drop down to cross Ripley Beck
before rising away outside the park wall, with a choice of paths.
Look back for a glimpse of the castle above the lake. This enclosed
track of Hollybank Lane rises to meet a broader track at a corner
of the park wall at Sadler Carr. In the trees in front is the site of
a medieval manor house, partly enclosed by a defensive moat. This
is clearly discerned from a little path venturing in just a few yards
ahead. Keep left a short way, and when the broader track swings
down to the left keep straight on a more inviting bridle-track. This
runs beneath fine oaks into Hollybank Wood. These glorious wood-
lands are perhaps at their finest when carpeted with bluebells.

Emerging at Holly Bank Lodge, advance along the narrow road, rising to meet the road in Clint. Your onward route takes a farm drive on the right, but first advance briefly straight on to see Clint Cross. Ancient stone tiers support a hollowed cross base, and old stocks stand alongside. The cross bears the inscription 'Palliser the Tailor', companion to an equally intriguing one at the start of WALK 19. Back on the farm drive this leads on past attractive Weavers Cottage to reach Clint Grange. After the first barn take a fence-stile on the left and resume parallel along the field edge. From a stile at the end slant left to a gate behind a track, and head up the large field, bearing slightly right to the corner of a wood.

Big views look over the Nidd Valley and over Harrogate to the Wolds. From a stile advance up the side of the wood and along its far side to a corner stile. Across it head right, angling away from the wood along a fenceside. After a couple of fields you approach the buildings at Whipley Hall. A small gate on the left just before the corner sees you bridge a tiny stream: resume along a paddock side to a small gate at the end onto the drive. Advance along this the short way to a surfaced fork, and bear right. This passes High Rails Farm to meet the estate wall. Remain on this same way past the attractive Park Lodge (1848 lintel). As a firmer track it shadows the park wall unfailingly back down to meet the outward route at Sadler Carr. Turn left back into Ripley.

*Clint Cross*

*3³⁄₄ miles
from Hampsthwaite*

**Delightful beckside,
parkland and riverbank
walking on the southern
slopes of the Nidd Valley**

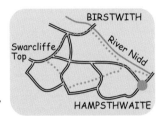

*Start* Village centre (GR: 259587), roadside parking
*Map* OS Explorer 298, Nidderdale

Hampsthwaite's focal point is an attractive green bearing
a village pump: close by are the Joiners Arms, Post office and
shops, while a graceful old bridge spans the Nidd. From the green
take the Birstwith road updale out of the village. After just a few
minutes it bridges Tang Beck: the intriguing inscription 'Palliser
the Hatter' is a twin of the 'Tailor' on Clint Cross (WALK 18).
Immediately over, take a stile on the left and head away upstream
along this broad, shallow valley. A splendid section traces the beck
tightly past Gormires Wood across it, through several fields to
ultimately emerge onto a back road. Cross straight over to a wall-
stile and resume. This time the valley takes some shape, and the
way slants up the bank to a gap-stile ahead. Advance to the next
stile in a hedge, and then follow a hedge away to a corner gate.
Here an enclosed grassy way runs on to join a drive at a house,
which leads out onto a road at a cottage and triangular green.

Turn right steadily uphill, and just beyond a junction
leave the road where it bends right. A wall-stile in the corner sends
you directly up the fieldside, rising to a ladder-stile in the very
corner. Continue rising the same way to a wall-stile at the top
corner onto another road. Turn right and down through a junction
at Meg Gate, down past the entrance to a school at the former
Swarcliffe Hall. Ahead is the unmistakable sight of the animal
feeds mill at Birstwith, while over to the right is the rather more
elegant tall spire of St James' church.

At the bottom bear right to the village store junction, where go left past the school on the main street towards the river. Across the bridge is the Old Station Inn. Before the river turn right towards the feed mill yard. The path is diverted to the left of the mill, so after crossing the mill-race on a footbridge, shadow the perimeter fence around above the river. At the end double back right with the fence, along to a kissing-gate back onto the original line of the path. Here turn left on a wallside path outside the trees, and from a stile at the end, rejoin the riverbank. This leads pleasantly downstream again, now for a considerable ramble. The point of leaving is at a bridle-gate back into a field, with a large barn up to the right: bear up to it, where a kissing-gate deposits you back onto the road. Note the character of this L-shaped old stable block, with an old mullioned window but a very modern roof.

Bear left along the road for Hampsthwaite, varying the entry into the village just after the church tower appears ahead.

Reaching a bend at the village sign, bear left along a gem of a part-flagged, leafy byway (an old church-goers' route from Birstwith) to emerge into the churchyard. The church of St Thomas a' Becket was much restored by the Victorians, but the tower is a good 500 years old. A path runs along the front of the church and out onto the village street, with the centre just to the right along Church Lane.

*Hampsthwaite church*

3³⁴ miles
from Birstwith

**The banks of the Nidd feature a stunning old bridge before more open rambling on the flanks**

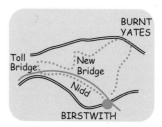

*Start* Village centre (GR: 243596), roadside parking
*Map* OS Explorer 298, Nidderdale

Dominated by a feeds mill, Birstwith is a colourful village with a shop, the Old Station Inn, and the elegant spired St James' church. Leave the road by heading upstream with a mill-cut by sports fields, running to a weir to trace the Nidd upstream. The path soon takes a straight hedge-side course rather than the river's gentle curve, rejoining it at the end for a super stroll to an old track just short of the beautiful arch of New Bridge. Dating from around 1615, it was rebuilt in 1822. From a stile on its near side resume upstream through two pathless riverside fields to a stile onto the valley road. Don't join the road but turn right on the Hartwith Mill private toll road. This crosses the quaint bridge to a red-brick cottage, an old rail building on the distinctive course of the old line. A minute further, leave the drive by a stile on the right, and follow a stream across to the old rail embankment. Pass through a wall-stile ahead and shadow the embankment to near the end, where a bridle-gate takes you over the scrub-choked line. In the slim pasture behind go left, back with the river. This broadens at a bridle-gate to lead back to a stile back at New Bridge.

Leave the river by going left along the enclosed old way embowered in greenery, soon re-crossing the rail line and rising delightfully between walls. Emerging at the top into a field, the now sunken way rises left up the side, soon re-entering its old guise at a gate above. A second grand section takes you further uphill: just after a stile on the left it levels out, here leave by a stile on the right. Cross the field to a gate onto a driveway at Dinmore House. Turn right down into the grounds and along between nice houses. In the yard cross to a gate ahead, along a garden and out via a gate/stile at the end. A super grassy path runs through colourful surrounds to a gate, where the path forks in a rough enclosure. Take the faint left option, rising to a gate beneath a barn.

Now ascend with the left-hand wall up three fields: the final stile puts you onto the B6165 at Burnt Yates. Turn right on the footway into the centre. On the left is the school, endowed in 1760. At the centre is St Andrew's church, while the Bay Horse pub is now a nursery. Burnt Yates straddles a broad ridge, and before leaving note a long view north-east to the North York Moors. Leave by a rough access road after the church, winding round to approach Church Farm at the end. Here take the track left to a gate/stile into a field. The Nidd Valley is again outspread. Follow the track dropping through a gate to fade at a bend: bear right on the grassy continuation along a hedgeside to meet a wall. It runs left with this to fade at a gate: note the solitary boulder in a field to the right. Through the gate head down the fieldside, transferring to the other side of the fence at a stile in a tiny wall. Descend pleasantly to a gate at the bottom, then bear right down to a corner gate onto a drive at West House. Turn down this onto suburban Nidd Lane, then left to Station Road on the edge of the village, going right to finish.

*New Bridge, near Birstwith*

# HILLSIDE GUIDES... cover much of Northern England

Other colour *Pocket Walks* guides (more in preparation)
·UPPER WHARFEDALE   ·LOWER WHARFEDALE
·MALHAMDALE   ·NIDDERDALE   ·AIRE VALLEY
·BOWLAND   ·HARROGATE & KNARESBOROUGH
·AMBLESIDE & LANGDALE   ·BORROWDALE

Our *Walking Country* range features more great walks...
·WHARFEDALE   ·MALHAMDALE   ·WENSLEYDALE
·HARROGATE & the WHARFE VALLEY  ·SWALEDALE
·RIPON & LOWER WENSLEYDALE   ·NIDDERDALE
·THREE PEAKS   ·HOWGILL FELLS
·TEESDALE   ·EDEN VALLEY   ·ALSTON & ALLENDALE

·NORTH YORK MOORS, SOUTH   ·HOWARDIAN HILLS

·ILKLEY MOOR   ·BRONTE COUNTRY   ·CALDERDALE
·PENDLE & the RIBBLE   ·WEST PENNINE MOORS
·ARNSIDE & SILVERDALE   ·LUNESDALE   ·BOWLAND

·LAKELAND FELLS, SOUTH   ·LAKELAND FELLS, EAST
·LAKELAND FELLS, NORTH   ·LAKELAND FELLS, WEST

Long Distance Walks
·COAST TO COAST WALK ·CUMBRIA WAY ·DALES WAY
·LADY ANNE'S WAY   ·NIDDERDALE WAY
·WESTMORLAND WAY   ·FURNESS WAY
·PENDLE WAY   ·BRONTE WAY   ·CALDERDALE WAY

Visit www.hillsidepublications.co.uk
or write for a catalogue